Taco
AND SQUIRREL

Run! Run! Run!
Bark! Bark! Bark!

Safe!
Safe!
Safe!

Bark!
Bark!
Bark!

climb!
Climb!
climb!
Snort!
Snort!
Snort!

Dig!
Dig!
Dig!

Holy Mackerel!!!!!!

WHO STOLE

OUR FOOD ?!?!?

CATS?

Hiss!
Hiss!
Hiss!

PIRATES?

Aargh !
Aargh!
Aargh!

ALIENS?

Beep!
Beep!
Beep!

I'm Hungry!

Me, too!

Do you want to look for our food together?
Yes! Yes! Yes!

HAVE YOU SEEN US?
BONE
-AND-
PEANUT
REWARD!!!
Good! Good! Good!

Nope. Sorry!
HAVE YOU SEEN US?
BONE
-AND-
PEANUT
REWARD!!!

Nope. Sorry!
HAVE YOU SEEN US?
BONE
-AND-
PEANUT
REWARD!!!

Nope. Sorry!
HAVE YOU SEEN US?
BONE
-AND-
PEANUT
REWARD!!!

Nope. Sorry!
HAVE YOU SEEN US?
BONE
-AND-
PEANUT
REWARD!!!

Yes!
Yes!
Yes!
HAVE YOU SEEN US?
BONE
-AND-
PEANUT
REWARD!!!
Where?
Where?
Where?

There!
There!
There!
HAVE YOU SEEN US?
BONE
-AND-
PEANUT
REWARD!!!

CROW!
LOLA!

ZOINKS!

Why did you take our food?

We were hungry!

We are, too!

Let's have a PICNIC!!!
YES!
YES!
YES!

Yum, Yum, Yum!
THE END

Taco,
Thank you for loving me and being the silliest, snuggliest, snortiest, snoringest, sweetest dog ever!

CPSIA information can be obtained at www.ICGtesting.com
Printed in the USA
BVIW12n1254311017
499164BV00006B/19

* 9 7 8 0 9 9 9 5 2 4 2 0 6 *